Midnight Zone

John Woodward

Heinemann Library
Chicago, Illinois

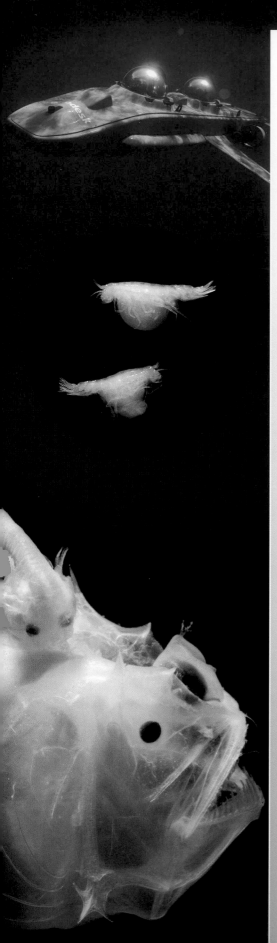

Consultant: Lundie Spence, PhD
Director, SouthEast Center for Ocean Sciences Education Excellence,
South Carolina Sea Grant Consortium

Produced by The Brown Reference Group plc
Project Editor: Tim Harris
Sub Editor: Tom Webber
Designer: Jeni Child
Picture Researcher: Sean Hannaway
Illustrator: Mark Walker
Managing Editor: Bridget Giles

Printed in China by WKT Company Limited

08 07 06 05 04
10 9 8 7 6 5 4 3 2 1

Library of Congress Cataloging-in-Publication data

Woodward, John, 1954-
   Midnight zone / John Woodward.
      v. cm. -- (Exploring the oceans)
Includes bibliographical references and index.
Contents: The black depths -- Your mission -- A midnight visitor -- The
big squeeze -- The big chill -- Lights in the dark -- Spotlights and
lures -- Loosejaws and fangtooths -- Weird and wonderful -- Mid-ocean
drive -- Looking for a giant -- Fins and tentacles -- Doomed liner --
Disaster detectives -- Rusting ruin -- Pacific dive -- A near miss --
Over the edge -- The challenger deep -- The deep water challenge --
Mission debriefing.
   ISBN 1-4034-5125-7 (hardcover) -- ISBN 1-4034-5131-1 (pbk.)
   1. Deep-sea ecology--Juvenile literature. 2. Oceanography--Juvenile
literature. [1. Deep-sea ecology. 2. Ecology. 3. Oceanography.] I.
Title.
   QH541.5.D35W66 2004
   551.46--dc22
                              2003021293

Acknowledgements

**The author and publishers are grateful to the following for permission
to reproduce copyright material:**
Front Cover: A deep-sea jellyfish in the midnight zone off Portugal (Paulo De Oliveira/Oxford
Scientific Films). **Back Cover:** Mark A Johnson/Corbis
p.1 David Shale/Nature Picture Library; p.2t Jay Wade/www.jaywade.com; p.2c Heather
Angel/Natural Visions; p.2b Clive Bromhall/Oxford Scientific Films; p.3 Karen Gowlett-Holmes/Oxford
Scientific Films; p.4 Heather Angel/Natural Visions; p.6-7 Norbert Wu/Oxford Scientific Films; p8–9
Jay Wade/www.jaywade.com; p.10 JPL/NASA; p.11 Norbert Wu/NHPA; p.12 Peter David/Natural
Visions; p.13 Julie Houck/Corbis; p.14b NOAA; p.14-15 Agence Nature/NHPA; p.16 Karen Gowlett-
Holmes/Oxford Scientific Films; p.16-17 Jeff Rotman/Nature Picture Library; p.18b Peter
David/Natural Visions; p.18–19 Clive Bromhall/Oxford Scientific Films; p.20 Heather Angel/Natural
Visions; p.21 Heather Angel/Natural Visions; p.22-23 Norbert Wu/NHPA; p.23b Peter David/Natural
Visions; p.24–25 Arctic Kingdom Marine Expeditions; p.26b David Shale/Nature Picture Library;
p.26–27 Peter David/Natural Visions; p.28 Peter David/Natural Visions; p.30b Ralph White/Corbis;
p.30–31 Ralph White/Corbis; p.32–33 Ralph White/Corbis; p.34–35 Ron Boardman, FPLA/Corbis;
p.35b Soc/Natural Visions; p.36-37 Ralph White/Corbis; p.37cr Captain Albert. E. Theberge/NOAA;
p.38–39 Peter David/Natural Visions; p.38br Peter Hvizdak, The Image Works/Topham; p.40 Heather
Angel/Natural Visions; p.42bl Keystone/Getty Images; p.42–43 JAMSTEC; p.44 David Shale/Nature
Picture Library.

Some words are shown in bold, **like this.** You can find
out what they mean by looking in the glossary.

Contents

The Black Depths

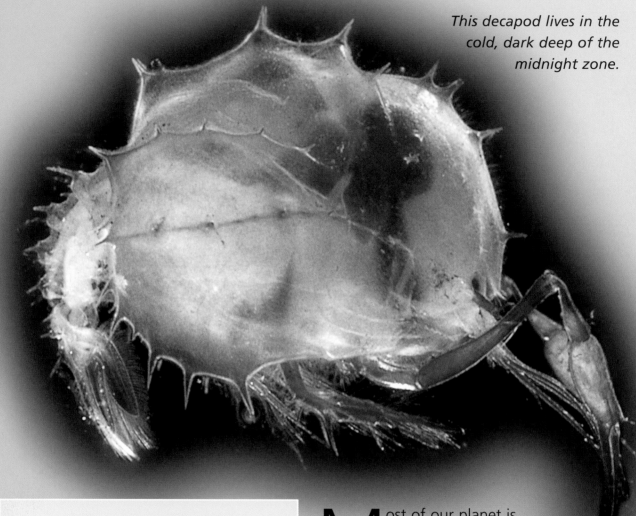

This decapod lives in the cold, dark deep of the midnight zone.

Deep ocean

How deep is the ocean? Think of it this way. The tallest building in America is the Sears Tower in Chicago, which is 1,454 feet (443 meters) tall. The average depth of the ocean is more than 11,500 feet (3,500 meters). So if eight Sears Towers were stacked on top of each other and stood on the ocean floor, they might just reach the surface. If you stood them in the bottom of the deepest ocean trench, the stack would need to be more than three times as high!

Most of our planet is covered by the huge areas of salt water that we call oceans. At the surface, these oceans can seem very different. Some, like parts of the South Pacific, are a clear, deep blue. Others, like much of the North Atlantic, are cloudy gray-green. Some areas of the oceans are warm and calm, while others are always cold and stormy. And in the polar regions, around the North Pole and around Antarctica, the ocean water at the surface is hidden beneath a layer of floating ice.

Deep below the surface, however, there are fewer differences between the oceans of the world. The water is always calm there. This is because the storm winds that whip up great waves have no effect on the water just 330 feet (100 meters) down. It is also cold because even in the **tropical** regions on either side of the **equator,** the Sun can warm up only the top 800 feet (240 meters) at most. Below this point a tropical ocean may be as cold as the water off Alaska or northern Europe.

Into the dark

The deep ocean also loses its color, because ocean water acts like a barrier to sunlight. Below about 600 feet (180 meters) from the surface, the only light is a faint blue glow, like the light you get at twilight. So this layer of the ocean, below the sunlit surface layer, is called the twilight zone. The blue glow gets steadily dimmer as you go deeper. In perfectly clear water there may be the faintest glimmer of blue light at 3,300 feet (1,000 meters). Then it fades altogether into inky blackness.

This is the midnight zone. It extends all the way down to the ocean floor, which lies more than 11,500 feet (3,500 meters) below the surface in midocean. So the midnight zone is more than twice as deep as the sunlit and twilight zones put together. In some places the ocean is even deeper. There are huge holes

Tidal Zone

Sunlit Zone

600 feet (180 meters)

Twilight Zone

3,300 feet (1,000 meters)

Midnight Zone You are Here

Seafloor

called trenches, in parts of the ocean floor. Some trenches are much deeper than 13,000 feet (4,000 meters). In places, the deepest trenches plunge to more than 33,000 feet (10,000 meters). These trenches are called the **hadal zone.** It is named for Hades, the underworld of the dead in ancient Greek mythology.

Much to learn

Altogether, these black depths make up about three-quarters of the world's ocean water. They account for more than half of the total living space on Earth! Yet we know very little about them. For every animal that we know about, there are probably 100 that we do not know.

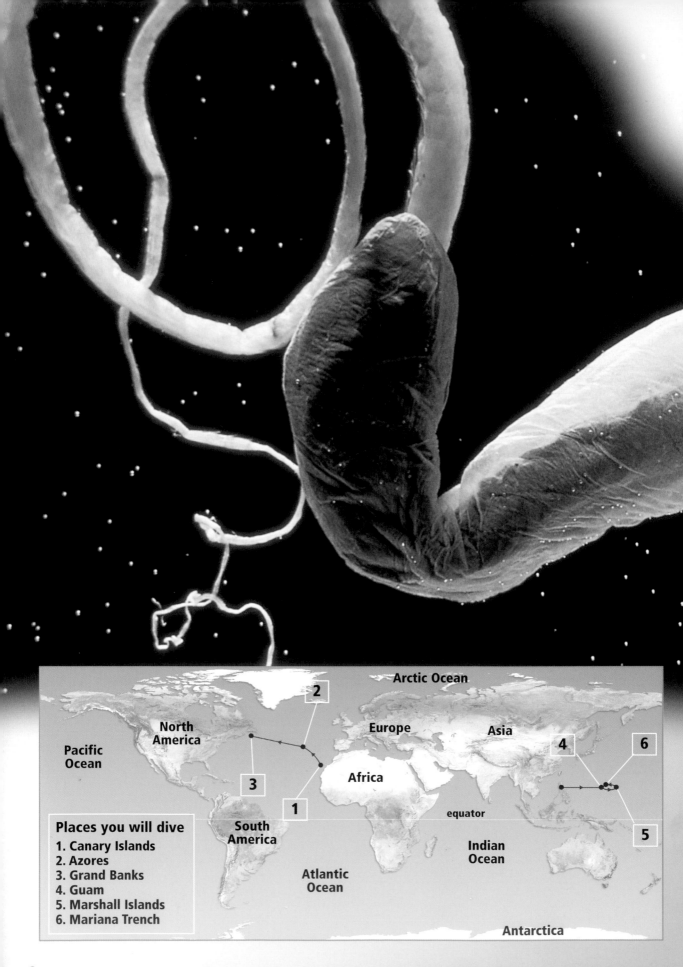

Places you will dive
1. Canary Islands
2. Azores
3. Grand Banks
4. Guam
5. Marshall Islands
6. Mariana Trench

Your Mission

You are going to help scientists explore the midnight zone. You will be using the most modern underwater craft. They are called **submersibles,** and they are equipped with powerful lights and cameras. They also have claws and diggers to take samples of water and animals. In a way submersibles are like spacecraft, because they allow a few people to explore regions that are as mysterious as the surface of Mars. They are also very costly to build.

Your journey starts in the Atlantic Ocean near the Canary Islands, off west Africa. There you will find out what it is like down in the midnight zone, and meet some of the weird animals that live there. You will investigate strange features like **bioluminescence** and discover how hunters find their **prey.**

Next you will travel across the Atlantic Ocean to the deep waters off the island of Newfoundland. There, you will dive down to look at a famous shipwreck that lies deep in the midnight zone. You will discover the strange things that can happen to metal objects in the deep ocean.

Then, you will move to the **tropical** Pacific, to compare its deep-sea world with the bleak north Atlantic. The Pacific is also ringed by deep ocean trenches. You will get the chance to explore the deepest trench of all, descending to the very bottom. It is the remotest place on Earth.

The deep-sea gulper eel lives in the midnight zone. It has hinged jaws and a stomach that stretches. Those features allow it to swallow animals bigger than itself.

The Deep Water Challenge

Throughout your mission to the midnight zone you will be using various types of **submersibles.** These craft must survive crushing **water pressures** and near-freezing temperatures. They also need to be able to move in any direction and measure depths and temperatures. Submersibles can take samples of rock and mud, and bring back clear pictures from the ocean depths. If they carry crew, they also need to carry supplies of air, food, and fresh water. Submersibles need to be comfortable so people can work in them for several hours.

So how do you build a submersible? The first thing you need is a pressure-proof chamber. The strongest shape for this is a thick metal ball, or **sphere.** Any doors are made so that the pressure squeezes them tightly shut. Windows are made of extremely thick, very tough plastic.

All the things that need air around them are put inside the main sphere. This includes the crew and all the electronic equipment. Extra spheres can hold air supplies for the crew. Anything made of solid metal is strong enough to survive the pressure. Equipment that will work in water can be put outside the sphere. This equipment may be protected by a shell of metal or plastic, which does not need to be as strong as the main sphere.

Streamlined shape helps submersible move quickly the through the water.

Powerful lights penetrate the darkness of the midnight zone.

Small electric motors called thrusters are hung on the outside. Some point forward and back, but others point sideways or up and down. Between them, they can push the submersible any way that the pilot wants. Mechanical arms on the front of the craft are able to collect samples and put them in a sample basket.

Crush-proof cameras

This still leaves some problems. What about lights? They have to be hung outside the submersible so they light

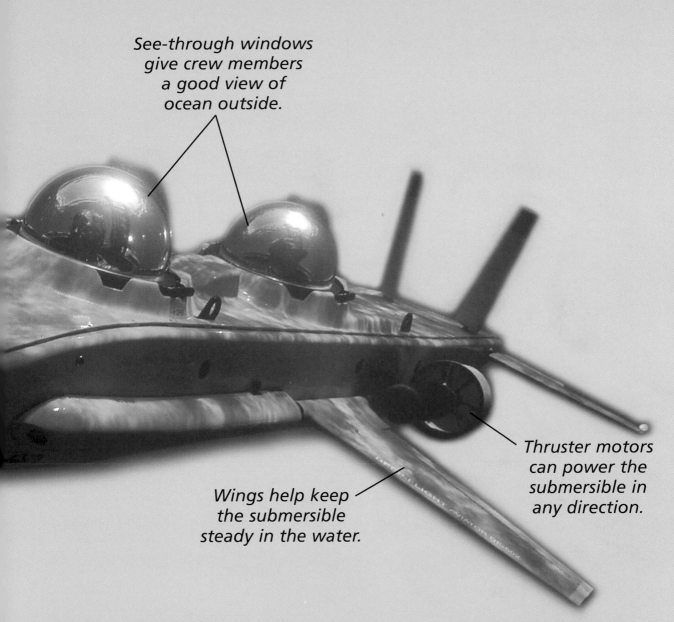

See-through windows give crew members a good view of ocean outside.

Thruster motors can power the submersible in any direction.

Wings help keep the submersible steady in the water.

up the water properly. But they work by electricity and contain gas, which can be squeezed by the water pressure. So lights have to be made extrastrong and waterproof. It is the same with cameras. An ordinary waterproof camera would be crushed by the pressure in the deep ocean.

Finally, the craft needs an escape system, in case something goes wrong. So the main sphere is usually able to break away from the rest of the craft and float back to the surface with the crew inside.

The only way to explore the midnight zone is in a submersible. It has several features that help you see what is happening in the dark ocean around you.

A Midnight Visitor

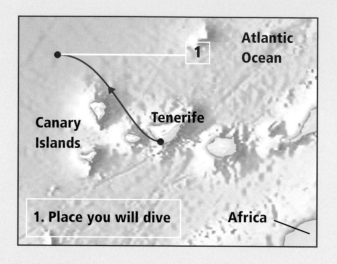

Atlantic Ocean

Canary Islands

Tenerife

1. Place you will dive

Africa

Tenerife is the tip of an extinct volcano that rises more than 23,000 feet (7,000 meters) from the floor of the Atlantic Ocean. Just a few miles north of the island, the water is 13,000 feet (4,000 meters) deep. So some fish that come to the surface at night could be coming all the way from the midnight zone.

You are going out to sea, too, but not on a fishing boat. You are joining the research ship *Aquarius.* The scientists on board are investigating the wildlife of the deep ocean, using a deep-water **submersible.** The scientists have asked you to join them, and you decide to go along.

It is dusk in a fishing port on Tenerife, one of the Canary Islands. Although it is still hot, there is a cool breeze blowing off the Atlantic Ocean. The boats are getting ready to spend the night fishing. The fishers here always catch more in the dark, because many deep-water fish come closer to the surface at night to feed.

This is Tenerife island seen from a satellite above Earth. The black area is ocean and the white patch is the top of a volcano.

Out at sea, you climb into the submersible and sit beside the pilot. The crew lower the craft over the back of the boat and down you go, into the ocean.

You can see shoals of fish feeding near the surface. They are lit up by the powerful lights of the submersible. You dive deeper and see some stranger fish. They live even deeper by day. Many of the fish glow with their own faint light. As you go deeper still, you see a big fish being attacked by a small shark. The shark pulls away as you get nearer, leaving a perfect circle-shaped

This is a cookie-cutter shark. It can swim as far as 2 miles (3 kilometers) down in the midnight zone.

wound in the fish's side. The attacker is a cookie-cutter shark. It feeds by slicing pieces out of bigger fish with its razor-sharp teeth. The shark swims away downward. Its belly glows with bright green light. You decide to follow.

The shark swims down and down. You check the depth, and discover that you have dived 3,300 feet (1,000 meters). You decide that you have gone deep enough, but the shark is still heading downward. It is your first contact with a creature from the midnight zone.

The Big Squeeze

Water is very heavy. Try lifting a 2-gallon (9-liter) bucket full of water. It is like lifting a bucket of rocks. If you think of an ocean as a giant bucket of water, you can see that it must be incredibly heavy. All that weight presses down on the ocean floor. The weight puts enormous **pressure** on anything that lives or goes there. It is like being squeezed in a giant press.

If you tried to dive into the midnight zone using an ordinary submarine, it would be crushed by the pressure of water. A submarine is fine in the sunlit zone near the surface, because there is not much water above the craft. Less water means less weight and pressure. But the deeper it goes, the more the water is squeezed.

During your dive near Tenerife, you measure the water pressure. At 33 feet (10 meters), the pressure is twice what it is at the surface. But at 3,300 feet (1,000 meters), the pressure is more than 100 times greater. If you were able to go down to the depth of the deepest ocean trenches, the pressure would be 1,000 times greater than at the surface.

Liquid protection

If the water pressure in the deep ocean could crush a submarine, how do animals like the cookie-cutter shark survive? The answer is that the bodies of deep-sea animals are mostly made of water. Water is a liquid, and you cannot crush a liquid. A pint or liter of liquid always takes up a

Spotted tinselfish like this one live near the top of the midnight zone.

Pressure proofing

The walls of a **submersible** have to be very strong to keep it from being crushed. The part you sit in (below) is shaped like a ball. A ball is the strongest shape. The chamber is made of extra-tough metal called titanium. The titanium is 2 inches (5 centimeters) thick, and the craft has plastic windows that are thicker than the walls of your house.

pint or liter of space, even if it is squeezed by extra-high pressure. So the water in an animal's body makes it pressure proof.

A submarine is full of air, which is a mixture of gases. Unlike liquids, gases can be squeezed, or **compressed,** so they take up less space. The air inside a submarine can be compressed by the water pressure outside. Compressed air takes up less space. So, if the metal walls of the submarine are not strong enough, they just burst inward.

The Big Chill

While you are measuring **water pressure** during your dive, you also measure the water temperature. Up near the surface the water is a warm 68 °F (20 °C). This is the temperature that most people set on their home central heating. But as you dive downward, the temperature drops.

At 660 feet (200 meters) your digital **thermometer** shows 59 °F (15 °C), which is still a comfortable temperature. At 1,000 feet (300 meters) it shows 45 °F (7 °C). The water has suddenly become a lot colder. You would not want to put your hand in water that cold, let alone go for a paddle! When you enter the midnight zone at 3,300 feet (1,000 meters), the thermometer shows you that the temperature is 39 °F (4 °C).

A small submersible is lowered over the side of a research ship.

The water gets a lot colder as you pass down through the twilight zone, between 600 feet (180 meters) and 1,000 feet (300 meters) deep. The water above the twilight zone (in the sunlit zone) is warmed by the sun. The colder water of the twilight zone mixes with the warmer water above. But below about 1,000 feet (300 meters), the mixing stops. Below that depth, the ocean is very cold. The boundary between the two layers is called a **thermocline.**

The water in the midnight zone is always cold, even in **tropical** oceans. Down near the ocean floor the water can be almost

*Spookfish live at great depths, where there is little light. They have upward-looking eyes. They can only see **prey** that is above them.*

freezing. The water temperature can even be slightly lower than 32 °F (0 °C), which is the normal **freezing point** of water. Salt water remains liquid at colder temperatures than fresh water. Because it is salty, ocean water has to be colder than fresh water to freeze.

Icy flow

There is another reason why the water in the midnight zone is so cold. In the oceans of the Arctic and Antarctic, water freezes at the surface and turns to floating ice. The very cold water underneath the ice sinks to the ocean floor. It then flows toward the **equator.** So a lot of the water in the midnight zone has come from the Arctic and Antarctic.

This movement of cold water is very useful. The icy water in the midnight zone stops tropical oceans from getting too hot. If the oceans were hotter, the air above them would be hotter, too. It would be too hot for people to live in the tropics. Also, the icy water carries oxygen that it **absorbed** when it was near the surface. Oxygen is one of the gases in air. We breathe oxygen. Even deep-ocean animals need it, so the icy flow keeps them alive.

Lights in the Dark

Some comb jellies live in very deep water. People can only see them in the dark midnight zone because they glow.

The day after your meeting with the cookie-cutter shark, you get the chance to dive deep into the midnight zone. Two of the scientists on board the research ship have planned a dive to 6,600 feet (2,000 meters). Since the **submersible** can carry three people, the crew can take you along.

At the top of the sunlit zone everything is brightly lit up. You can see all the colors of the fish. As you go deeper the light gets dimmer and turns blue. You cannot see colors other than shades of blue. When you eventually reach the midnight zone there seems to be no light at all. And yet you know the sun is still shining on the ocean's surface.

Glowing in the gloom

You peer out at the black water through the thick windows of the submersible. The scientists have not switched on the submersible's lights. Then a strange, glowing object appears in the water. It is a deep-water jellyfish. Its round body is lit up with red and blue lights.

These two deep-sea squid are about as long as a man's hand.

The lights of the jellyfish blink out as it drifts away, so maybe it lit up because the submersible was close by.

You see some more lights. You cannot make out what they are, but suddenly a different kind of jellyfish switches on its lights right in front of you. As you watch, some of its **tentacles** fall off and drift away in the water. They are still glowing, but the jellyfish itself has disappeared.

Then you realize it is not the tentacles glowing, but a fish eating the tentacles. The jellyfish seems to have dropped the glowing tentacles so it can escape the hungry fish. During your trip you also see a deep-water squid squirt a **luminous** cloud into the water before swimming away. All these animals seem to be using light to confuse their enemies.

Living light

The light made by jellyfish and other living things is called **bioluminescence.** It usually works by mixing oxygen with chemicals called luciferin and luciferase. This happens inside the animals' **photophores.** By controlling how the substances are mixed, the animal can make its lights flash on and off. This is how fireflies, which are really beetles, make their light.

Spotlights and Lures

As you watch the strange lights in the black water, you have trouble seeing what is happening. Many of the animals are not lit up all over their bodies. You cannot see what they are.

The scientists have an answer to this. They switch on a very small spotlight. This lights up the animals, and you can still see their natural glow. Suddenly you are able to figure out what is going on.

Red for danger

You realize that a small red light in front of your window is part of a fish. The fish has long, scary-looking teeth. It is a dragonfish. The fish has a red light below each eye that it uses to hunt its **prey.** The dragonfish feeds mainly on red shrimp, which are lit up by the red light. The shrimp cannot see anything red, but the dragonfish can. By lighting the shrimp with its red lights, the dragonfish can see without scaring its prey away.

Dragonfish have rows of red lights. They use these to find their next meal.

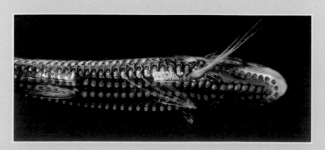

lure

This large female anglerfish has two small males attached to its side.

Some time later you see another weird light. This one is a pale, eerie blue. When you point the spotlight at it, you see that the blue light is being carried by an ugly black fish. The light is on the end of a long rod sticking out of the fish's head. The light is just above its big, long-toothed mouth.

This fish is a deep-sea anglerfish. It is using the light as a **lure.** Any other fish that are attracted to the light are likely to swim within easy range of the anglerfish's teeth. If they do that, the anglerfish snaps them up. Attracting prey like this is a good idea, because there are very few fish that live at these depths. Finding them without light is very difficult.

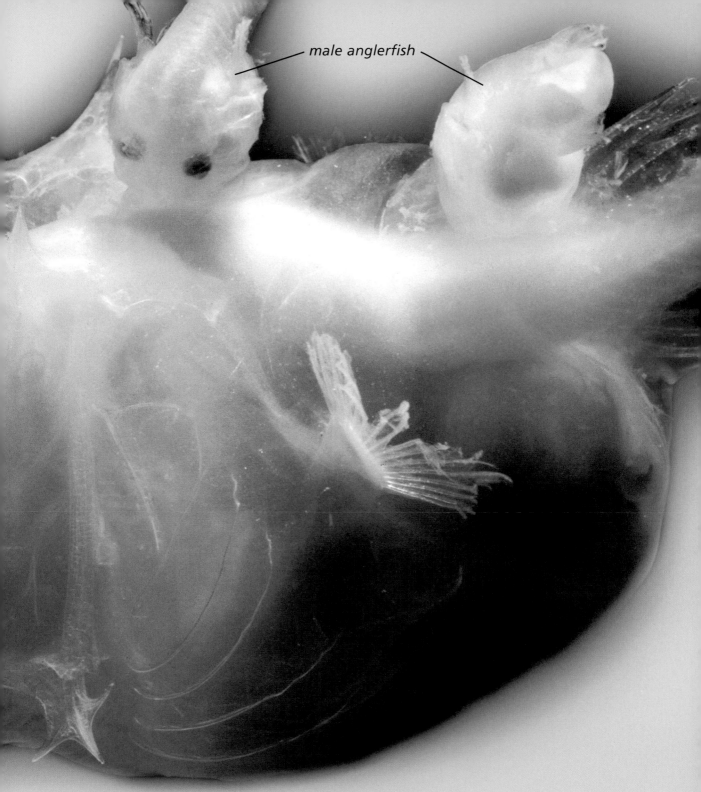

male anglerfish

Strange anglers

The anglerfish's light is unusual because it is produced by **bacteria** that live inside the lure. The fish supplies the bacteria with food, and the bacteria make the light. They are **bioluminescent.** When **organisms** help each other like this, it is called a **mutualism.** Anglerfish are unusual for another reason. Those with lures are all females. The males are much smaller than the females. The males attach themselves to the females with their teeth. The male's body grows into the female's. He gets all his food from her blood.

A fangtooth's teeth are so big it cannot close its mouth. This fish snacks on small fish and shrimp.

Loosejaws and Fangtooths

During your deep dive near Tenerife, you spend around three hours in the midnight zone. During that time you see very few fish. This is partly because it is difficult to see very far. But mostly it is because fish are very uncommon in the deep, dark water. There is not enough food for fish to live in big groups (schools). They are usually spread out with a lot of clear water between them.

This means that the hunters, or **predators,** get very few chances to kill and eat **prey.** The predators have to make sure that nothing they catch is able to escape. This explains why so many of them have huge mouths and very long teeth, like needles. They have been given names like "fangtooths" and "rat-trap fish."

Huge appetites

Some dragonfish are called loosejaws. They can open their mouth extra-wide to gulp down animals that are bigger than their own head. Many fish also have an elastic stomach that can stretch like a balloon. So they can swallow victims that are even bigger than their own body!

The fish are much smaller than you expected. The pictures that you saw before your deep dive made them look like sea monsters, but most of the real fish are only a few inches long. They have big teeth and

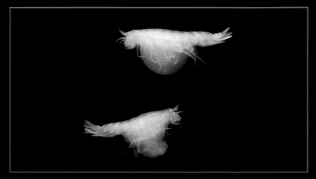

These tiny amphipods are related to crabs. They look swollen because they have just eaten a meal.

jaws, but their bodies are tiny. They have weak, flabby muscles and small fins. They do not look like they could swim far.

Many of the fish that live in the deep ocean, where food is hard to find, are small. A fish with a big body needs more food to keep it alive. So if food is hard to find, it is likely to die. Fish with smaller bodies are able to survive for longer without a meal—especially if they can eat a huge meal when they get the chance.

Amphipods

Millions of crustaceans called amphipods live in the midnight zone. They eat bits of dead animals that drift down through the ocean. Scientists have found amphipods even in a very deep trench, 35,000 feet (10,600 meters) beneath the ocean surface.

Weird and Wonderful

As you start the return trip to the surface, you spot something much bigger than the other fish that you have been looking at. Yet it is very hard to make out what it can be. It looks like a giant mouth, with no body at all. It looks like a nightmare.

Your scientist friends get very excited, because they have never seen one of these alive before. It is a gulper eel. Its long, slender black-skinned body is almost invisible in the dark water. Your lights show only its huge jaws and a pair of tiny eyes that seem to be perched on the end of its nose.

As you watch, the gulper eel opens its mouth. You can see how it got its name. Its jawbones are extremely long. They stretch the skin of its mouth open like a big black bag. As well as a very big mouth, the animal has an elastic, stretchy stomach. It is as long as an adult person is tall. Since the eel is much bigger than most other midnight zone fish, it can gulp down almost anything it finds.

Feeling in the dark

Gulper eels have deep-water relatives that are almost as weird. They are called saccopharyngid (sac-O-far-in-gid) eels. They look a bit like gulper eels, but their mouth is not as big. Saccopharyngid eels can grow even longer than gulper eels. They have a luminous tail that glows with red, pink, and blue light.

These eels have bumps on their sides that contain sense organs. They detect tiny changes in the **water pressure** around them. These changes are often made by other fish swimming by in the dark. So the eel can sense when a fish is nearby, even though it cannot see it. It probably

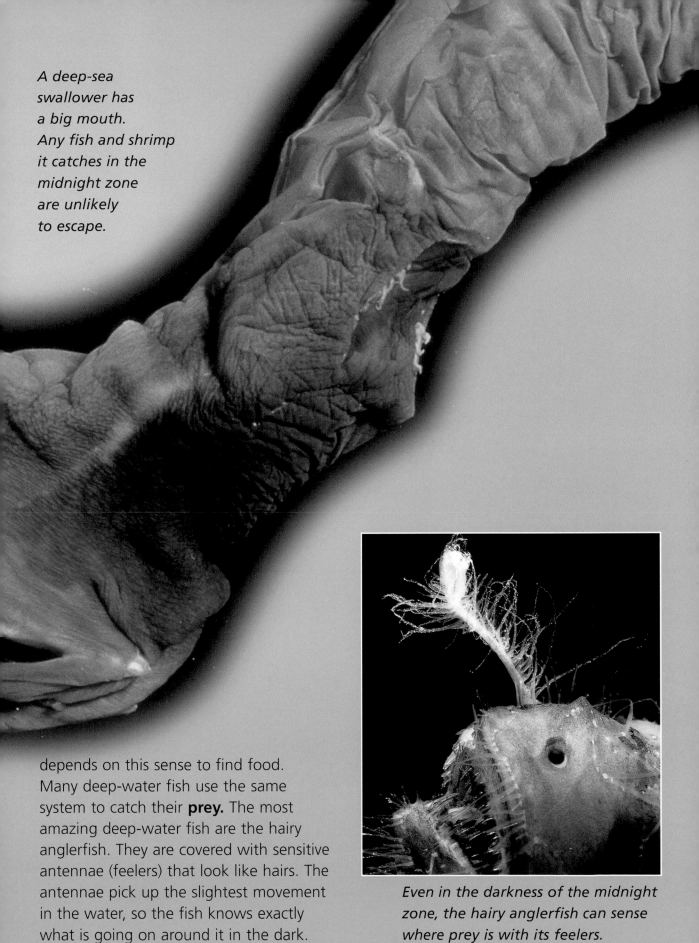

*A deep-sea
swallower has
a big mouth.
Any fish and shrimp
it catches in the
midnight zone
are unlikely
to escape.*

depends on this sense to find food.
Many deep-water fish use the same
system to catch their **prey.** The most
amazing deep-water fish are the hairy
anglerfish. They are covered with sensitive
antennae (feelers) that look like hairs. The
antennae pick up the slightest movement
in the water, so the fish knows exactly
what is going on around it in the dark.

*Even in the darkness of the midnight
zone, the hairy anglerfish can sense
where prey is with its feelers.*

Midocean Dive

When you finish your dive near the Canary Islands, you relax while the research ship *Aquarius* heads northwest across the Atlantic Ocean toward Canada. *Aquarius* is leaving the warm **tropics** and moving into the cool northern Atlantic Ocean.

On the way, you stop for a while in the Azores Islands. These islands lie on the Mid-Atlantic Ridge. This is a chain of underwater mountains that runs down the middle of the Atlantic. The scientists have planned a dive in the **submersible,** and you are going, too.

Deep sleeper

The submersible goes down to 6,600 feet (2,000 meters) to see what lives in the water above the ridge. As you expected, there are more of the lit-up fish with long teeth here. But then something much bigger comes into view. It swims toward a dragonfish and swallows it whole. It is a shark.

You have already seen sharks in the shallow water of the sunlit zone. It seems odd to see one so deep. Yet the first midnight zone fish you saw was the little cookie-cutter shark. This is one of its relatives, called the sleeper shark. It is about as long as two cars parked fender to fender. It is the largest fish known to live in the midnight zone.

How can such a big fish live in a place where there is so little food? The little cookie-cutter shark gives a clue, because you first saw it in much shallower water. Sharks seem able to move up and down in the ocean more easily than other fish. Sharks can visit different zones to hunt. Sleeper sharks often hunt near the surface in the far north. There, Inuit hunters sometimes catch them through holes in the ice. Sleeper sharks seem to like cold water. In **tropical** regions, they favor the cold, dark midnight zone.

Shark senses

Sharks are able to hunt in the dark because they have a great sense of smell. So do lots of animals. But sharks also have a very unusual sense. They can sense the tiny electrical signals made by other animals. If a shark is hunting nearby, it is likely to make other animals nervous. They will produce more signals. So, the shark will have a better chance of finding them. The system works very well. Scientists call this sense the shark's electrosense.

Looking for a Giant

One of the scientists diving with you in the **submersible** is an expert on deep-sea squids and their relatives. She is hoping to be the first scientist to see a live giant squid and find out where it hunts. She knows that giant squid live in the area, because a dead one was recently hauled up in a fishing net. So after watching the sleeper shark for a while, you move off to look for a giant squid.

A giant squid can grow to 60 feet (18 meters) long. This includes its extra-long tentacles. It has the largest eyes of any animal. The eyes are as wide across as dinner plates! The squid must use these huge eyes to hunt its **prey** by sight. So, maybe the squid lives in the twilight zone, where there is just a little light in the water. Or maybe it hunts lit-up animals in the midnight zone. No one knows for sure.

You cruise around in the dark, hoping for a lucky break. You will need luck, because you have no way of knowing where a giant squid might be feeding. And unlike many of the animals that it eats, a giant squid does not light up.

Brilliant disguise

You see other animals. There are many shrimp feeding on little bits of food sinking through the water. The shrimp look brilliant red when the submersible's lights shine on them. In the midnight zone, their red color actually helps hide them. It is a kind of **camouflage.** That is because most of the natural light down here is the blue glow made by **bioluminescence.** In blue light, a red shrimp looks black, just like the water around it. The shrimp are visible only to dragonfish, with their red lights, and to people in submersibles.

Many deep-water animals do not hunt by sight. As you watch, a glowing jellyfish called *Periphylla* (pe-ree-PHI-la) drifts by and catches a red shrimp in its stinging tentacles. The jellyfish finds its prey by luck and by feel. It is having more luck finding prey than you are finding a giant squid.

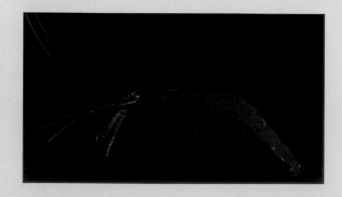

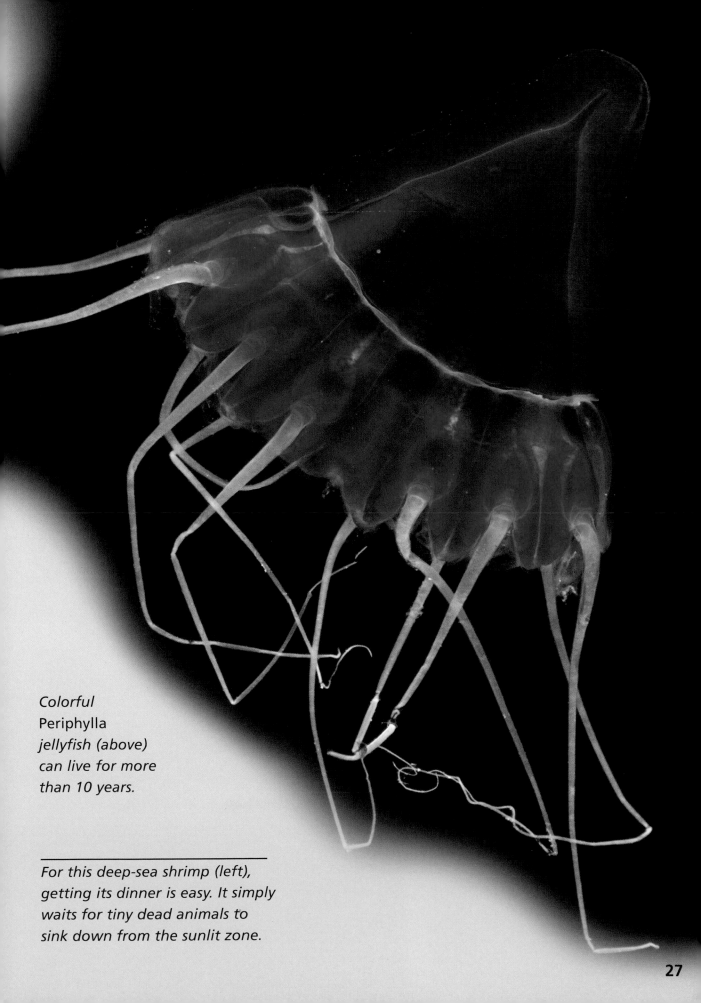

Colorful Periphylla jellyfish (above) can live for more than 10 years.

For this deep-sea shrimp (left), getting its dinner is easy. It simply waits for tiny dead animals to sink down from the sunlit zone.

This deep-sea squid is called Bolitaenia. Its large eyes give it a good view of everything around it. The squid can see food and enemies.

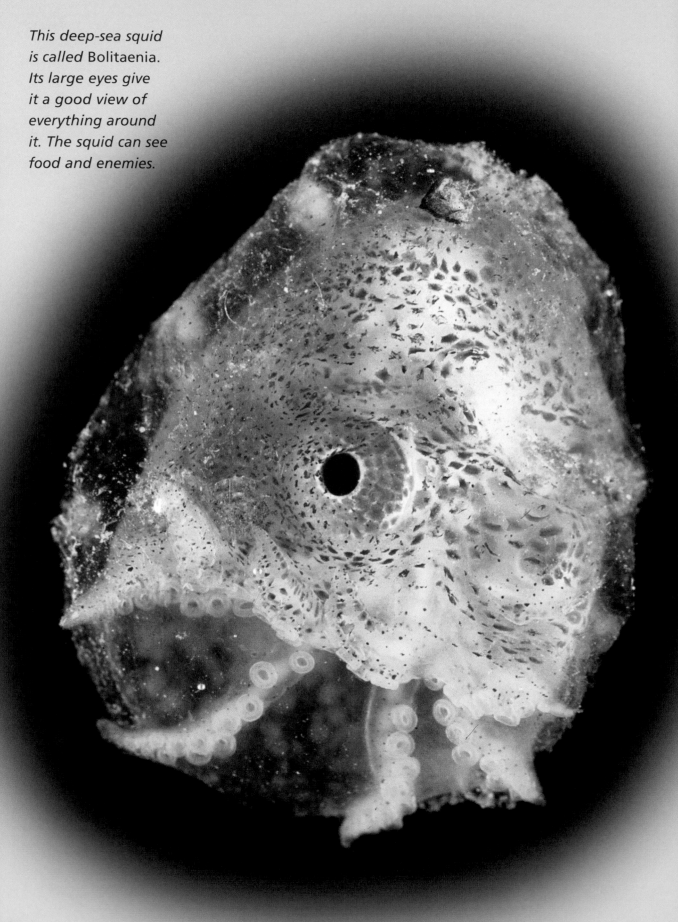

Fins and Tentacles

Your squid expert is having no luck finding a giant squid off the Azores. But there are plenty more squid in the sea. They are among the most common deep-sea animals, and they come in all sizes. Some squid are very large, and others are tiny creatures just an inch (2.5 centimeters) long. They have eight arms with strong suckers, and two long tentacles. Squid use their tentacles to catch fish and other **prey.**

As you cruise through the midnight zone, you see several different kinds of squid. Most of them are small. They have small arms and move slowly. Many just seem to hang in the water. They wait for prey to drift close. Then they grab it with their tentacles. But then you see something that is very different.

It is certainly a squid, but it has two broad fins, like wings. It also has amazingly long, thin arms. It is pushing itself along backward as squid often do.

Its long arms are trailing behind it like fishing lines. The whole animal is about 23 feet (7 meters) long. It is an exciting find, because these animals were only discovered late in 2001. They have not been given a name, yet.

Sticky umbrellas

A little later you see some animals that look like squid to you. But your expert tells you that they are finned octopuses. Octopuses are similar to squid but they do not have the pair of tentacles.

Most octopuses live among rocks in the sunlit zone. But these finned octopuses live much deeper in the ocean. Their eight arms are joined by thin sheets (webs) of skin. When an octopus stretches its arms out it looks a bit like an umbrella. Each octopus hangs in the water. It slowly beats its fins to create a gentle **current** around its body. The current pushes small animals into its "umbrella." There they stick to the gluey **mucus** around the octopus's mouth.

Speedy squid and octopuses

Squid and octopuses are mollusks. Snails and clams are also mollusks. Squid and octopuses are active and intelligent creatures. They push themselves along by squirting water out of their body. Some squid can swim very fast. In the sunlit zone, there are squid that can even shoot out of the water and fly through the air!

Doomed Liner

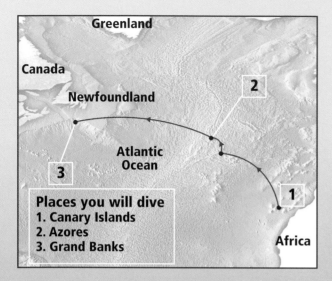

Places you will dive
1. Canary Islands
2. Azores
3. Grand Banks

Map labels: Greenland, Canada, Newfoundland, Atlantic Ocean, Africa

People rarely visit the midnight zone. However, plenty of things that have been made by people find their way down there. Ships that are wrecked at the surface sink through the layers of the ocean to rest on the ocean floor. You are going to visit the most famous of these shipwrecks: the *Titanic*.

In 1912 the *Titanic* was the most magnificent ocean liner in the world. It was brand new and making its first voyage across the Atlantic Ocean from England to the United States. Just before midnight on Sunday, April 14th, the *Titanic* hit an iceberg. An iceberg is a giant lump of frozen ocean. The iceberg had drifted south from the Arctic. The ice cut into the side of the ship, which slowly filled with water and sank. Only 705 people survived out of 2,200 passengers and crew. The *Titanic* sank 453 miles (725 kilometers) southeast of Newfoundland. The ship was just a few miles south of the Grand Banks.

The Grand Banks is a region of ocean that is only about 1,000 feet (300 meters) deep. Instead, the *Titanic* sank through 12,500 feet (3,840 meters) of water. That is well into the midnight zone.

Dangerous work

It takes more than three days to reach the wreck site from the Azores, so you have plenty of time to learn about it. The wreck was discovered in September, 1985, by people using remote controlled underwater video cameras. They found the ship had broken into two parts. It was lying almost upright on the seafloor amid a mass of junk.

Exploring a shipwreck is very dangerous, because it is easy to get trapped inside the rusty shell. It can also collapse on top of you.

Thousands of feet above the Titanic, *your* **submersible** *is ready to be lowered into the ocean.*

The bigger the wreck, the more dangerous it is, and the *Titanic* is one of the biggest. So although you are going to go down to the wreck in the submersible, you will use a remotely operated vehicle, or **ROV,** to look inside it.

The wreck of the Titanic*. The shapes that look like rusty icicles are called* **rusticles.**

Remotely operated vehicle (ROV)

Your ROV is a box-shaped submarine just 16 inches (40 centimeters) square. That is no bigger than a computer screen. The ROV is fitted with its own motors and video cameras. The driver, or pilot, of the submersible controls the ROV from inside the submersible. Electrical signals are sent through a thin cable. This allows the ROV to move around inside the junk-filled wreck.

Disaster Detectives

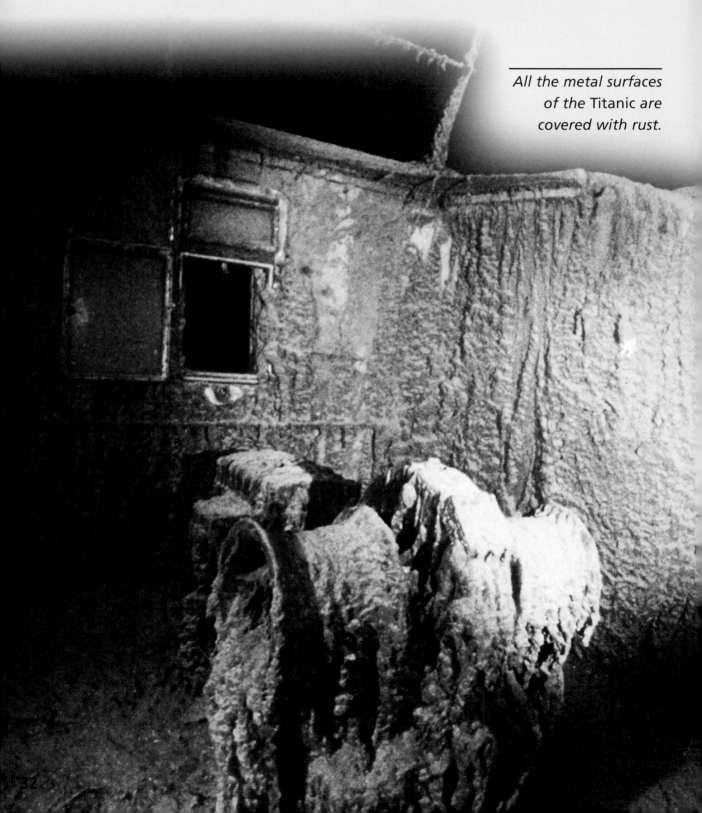

All the metal surfaces of the Titanic are covered with rust.

When you arrive over the wreck site, there is not much to see. It is midsummer, so there are no dangerous icebergs. You climb into the **submersible** and start the long dive to the wreck. It is nearly 2.5 miles (4 kilometers) below the ocean surface.

It takes two-and-a-half hours to get there. For most of that time you are diving in the dark. First, you pass through the sunlit zone. The surface water is thick with **plankton** around Newfoundland, and this makes the water very cloudy. The sunlight cannot pass through the water easily. Then you drop through the twilight zone, which is almost totally dark. Finally, you go down through the midnight zone. Here, the water has very little plankton, because most plankton cannot survive where there is no light.

When you get close to the ocean floor, the pilot switches on the powerful headlights and heads for the wreck. Suddenly, in front of you, is the great ship itself.

Into the wreck

The submersible rises up over the railings at the front of the ship. Growing from the wreck are long, rusty spines called **rusticles.** You use the submersible's mechanical hand to snap off some rusticles and put them in the sample basket. Then the submersible heads toward the ship's **bridge.** That is where the captain, Edward J. Smith, would have stood as it sank.

This is where you need the **ROV.** Using remote video, you guide the ROV through the *Titanic*'s smashed windows. You see the remains of one of the ship's three steering wheels, and imagine it being turned frantically to avoid the iceberg. The crew of the *Titanic* saw the iceberg too late. They could not avoid it. You send the ROV deep into the ship. It is heading for the part of the ship that hit the ice.

Eventually it gets there. You can see how the ship's steel plates have been bent. There is no big hole in the side of the ship, just a few narrow slits. Altogether the slits cover just 12 square feet (1.1 square meters). So all the water that sank this huge luxury liner must have come in through a hole no bigger than a bathtub.

Rusting Ruin

To get out of the *Titanic,* the **ROV** has to go back the way it came in. Its motors have stirred up a lot of the mud lying on the wreck. That makes the water cloudy. It becomes hard to steer the ROV using remote video. Once you have got the ROV back, you decide to take a closer look at the mud. The mud is called sediment.

You can see some big stones with sharp, broken edges. They are not the rounded stones you normally find at sea. They are stones that were frozen within **glaciers** in the Arctic. Icebergs broke off the glaciers. The icebergs floated far out into the ocean. When the icebergs eventually melted, the stones sank quickly to the ocean floor. Some stones landed here, on a ship that was sunk by an iceberg.

Most of the sediments are made of muddy stuff, not stones. That was the mud stirred up by the ROV's propellers. You use the **submersible's** sampler to gather some of the mud. Then you start the long trip back to the surface.

Iron eaters

When you return to the research ship, you examine the **rusticles** that you collected from the wreck of the *Titanic.* The rusticles look like dripping, rust-colored candle wax. You slice some up, and look at the slices under a powerful **microscope.** What you see is amazing. The rusticles are full of tiny **bacteria.** They have made themselves a home in the rust, a bit like a tiny termite mound.

Tiny creatures called foraminiferans build themselves homes from chalk. When they die, the shell of their home drifts to the ocean floor. This foraminiferan shell has been magnified around 250 times.

Next you examine the fine sediments that you collected. They look like flour. You put some under the microscope. Most are tiny sand grains, but there are also some things that look like shells. They are not really shells at all, but the remains of dead **plankton.** They have drifted down through the ocean like snow, to settle on the wreck. Most of the sand grains were dumped on the wreck in 1929. That year a huge slump of sand came down the slope from the shallow Grand Banks to the deep ocean floor where the *Titanic* rests.

Marine snow (below) looks like very small snowflakes. It is little bits of dead plankton that have been stuck together with a sugary gel. The gel is produced by bacteria.

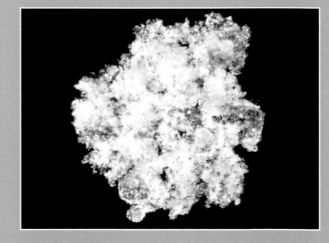

It seems that the deep-sea bacteria are taking iron from the wreck of the *Titanic* and "eating" it. Eventually the bacteria will eat so much iron that the giant wreck will collapse into a heap of rusty sludge.

Pacific Dive

You have spent a lot of time looking at the midnight zone of the Atlantic Ocean. For the next part of your mission you take a long-haul flight to the other side of the world. You are joining an ocean research team in the western Pacific.

You land at Manila in the Philippines, and then travel east to the island of Guam. The ocean world here is quite unlike the chilly North Atlantic. Here, the water is a beautiful clear blue. Colorful **corals** grow in the warm sunlit zone. But you are not here to look at coral. You have come to visit the midnight zone.

Guam is the home of an American military base. The United States Navy is testing two new deep-water **submersibles** in the ocean nearby. One submersible is a large craft that can stay below for several days. The other submersible has been built to explore the bottom of the deepest ocean trench on the planet.

Across the abyss

You have been invited to join the test team of the large submersible. The team is planning a three-day trip across the Mariana Abyssal Plain, near Guam. Abyssal means "very deep." The plain is 20,000 feet (6,000 meters) below the surface. It is surrounded by extinct underwater volcanoes called **seamounts.** Some of these rise above the ocean surface and form islands. Other seamounts are not tall enough to reach the surface. They are invisible from above the water. Many have never been mapped on an ocean chart.

There are often pillowlike rocks around seamounts. The rocks are called pillow lavas. They form when volcanoes erupt underwater. When the red-hot rock (lava) meets the very cold water it quickly gets hard.

Places you will dive
1. Guam
2. Marshall Islands
3. Mariana Trench

Pacific Ocean

2

3

● Manila

Philippines

1

New Guinea

As you dive through the sunlit zone of the ocean you are dazzled by the beauty of the **tropical** Pacific. There are groups, or shoals, of brightly colored fish. You see them being chased by powerful tuna and sleek dolphins.

As you go deeper, the water gets darker and colder. Everything looks dark blue. There is very little light. This is the twilight zone. Then it is totally dark. When you get to 16,400 feet (5,000 meters), it seems just just like the north Atlantic Ocean again. The water is almost at the freezing point. Even the weird deep-sea animals look a little like those you saw in the North Atlantic. It seems that the midnight zone is much the same, wherever you go in the world's oceans.

This diagram shows how a seamount rises from the ocean floor. The flat area around the seamount is called an abyssal plain.

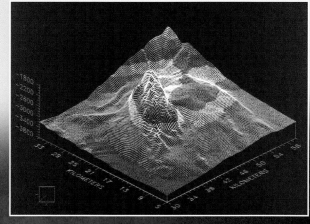

A Near Miss

You return to the surface and get on board the U.S. Navy ship. The captain steers the ship toward the Marshall Islands, 1,200 miles (1,900 kilometers) to the east. There, you dive again in the **submersible.** The map shows nothing in the area except empty ocean. But you never know what you will find in the midnight zone.

The submersible is guided by **sonar.** Sonar tells you the shape of the ocean floor and anything that may lie in the way. The sonar signals are fed to a computer. The computer shows a picture of your surroundings on a very big screen. Watching the screen is like looking out of a window at the deep ocean world.

Heavy rock

Suddenly most of the screen changes color, from deep blue to gray. It is a great wall of rock, rising up from the ocean floor. The

This is a rat-tail fish. There are probably more rat-tail fish in the oceans than there are people in the world.

chart is wrong. You have discovered a new **seamount.** The captain stops the submersible and heads slowly upward to see how high it is. Meanwhile, you go to the front of the craft and look out through one of its very thick windows.

Sonar

Sonar works by sending pulses of sound through the water. When each pulse hits something, it bounces back. The longer it takes to do this, the farther it has traveled. Whales use this system to find their way through the water. The scientist (right) is watching sonar pictures on a computer screen.

Lit up by the powerful lights, the rock looks dark and dangerous. It is made up of rounded, tumbled shapes, like pillows. As the submersible gets closer, you use its grasping tool to gather a rock sample. When you get the sample on board, you find it is very heavy and almost black. You have seen this type of rock before, on the Azores. It is called **basalt.** It is the volcanic rock that forms most of the ocean floor.

Looking out through the window, you see some strange fish with long, thin tails. They are feeding among the tumbled rocks, or pillow lavas. The fish are rat-tails. They are not the only living things in the black water. You can also see sea anemones and many slim sea stars with feathery arms. They are called brittle stars. But investigating this seafloor life will have to wait until your next mission.

Over the Edge

After investigating the **seamount,** the captain of the **submersible** decides to head north to see if there are any more. You spend a day doing this, and discover three more seamounts that no one knew existed. Then you return to the surface and join the navy ship once more. The captain turns the ship around, back toward Guam, which is now about 250 miles (400 kilometers) away. The journey will take at least 12 hours, so you decide to get some sleep while the crew carries on.

When you wake up, you find that the ship is about to cross the Mariana Trench. This is one of the deep holes in the floor of the Pacific Ocean. It—and others like it—form in places where the rocks of the ocean floor are sinking into the interior of Earth.

You dive in the submersible once more. It descends to a depth of 18,000 feet (5,500 meters). The computer screen shows the ocean floor in pale gray, 1,500 feet (450 meters) below you. But then the screen starts getting darker. The figures showing the depth increase rapidly. The ocean floor is falling away.

Soon the **sonar** shows a depth of 25,000 feet (7,600 meters). This is deeper than the submersible can go. But the captain

This ostracod lives in the midnight zone. Ostracods are relatives of crabs and shrimp. This female is carrying eggs. They are visible beneath her skin.

decides to explore the trench anyway. He will stop when the water pressure reaches the limit of safety.

Into the hadal zone

When you sink below 20,000 feet (6,000 meters), you enter a layer of the ocean called the **hadal zone.** Very few people have been this deep. As you go lower, the submersible's lights pick out more animals. There are brittle stars and rat-tails like the ones you saw on the seamount. You see a chimaera, which is a weird-looking relative of sharks. It has big green eyes. And there is a strange big-headed fish called a sea snail. These animals live mainly on scraps that sink down from the ocean above.

When you are 22,000 feet (6,700 meters) below the surface, the **water pressure** alarm sounds inside the submersible. You cannot go any deeper. There are a few lit-up deep-water fish. There are not many, though, because food is very hard to find this deep in the ocean.

You set off across the deep trench, heading for the other side. Just here the trench is about 100 miles (160 kilometers) wide. It would take almost two hours to travel that distance in a car on a highway. But in the submersible it would take a lot longer. It has been a long day, and you have seen a great deal. You are feeling tired and so is the captain of the submersible. He decides to take it back up to the surface. There you will join the waiting navy ship again

The Challenger Deep

The navy ship returns to the island of Guam. You get back there in time to join an expedition to the deepest part of the Mariana Trench. It is about 200 miles (320 kilometers) southwest of the island. The deepest place is called the Challenger Deep. It is named for the British survey ship *Challenger II,* which discovered the trench in 1951.

The bottom of the ocean

In 1960, the U.S. Navy sent a **submersible** called *Trieste* into the Challenger Deep to see just how deep it was. The submersible had a crew of two people. The deepest they got was 35,813 feet (10,916 meters). That is more than twice the average depth of the ocean floor. And it is deeper than the highest land mountain, Everest, is tall.

At this depth, the **water pressure** is 16,000 pounds per square inch (1,125 kilograms per square centimeter). That is

The submersible Trieste *(left) after it had been to the bottom of the Challenger Deep in 1960. Sailors from the U.S. Navy are rowing out to meet the crew.*

The crew of a Japanese submersible on its way into the midnight zone.

lowers the submersible into the water well before dawn. You join the captain of the submersible on the long dive.

Into the Challenger Deep

It takes more than 6 hours to dive through nearly 7 miles (11 kilometers) of water. It seems even longer. Cramped inside the cabin, you feel like an astronaut on a mission to the Moon.

Eventually the instruments show that you are getting near the bottom. The pilot of the submersible slows the dive rate so you are sinking very slowly. You hear a slight crunch, and feel the craft settle on the floor of the ocean trench. You are in the deepest hole on Earth.

You switch on the outside lights and peer through the extra-thick window. Thick, pale brown slime lies on the ocean floor, forming an almost flat layer as far as you can see. But it is not completely flat. There are small mounds and hollows, and strange grooves. The grooves are probably the tracks of animals called sea cucumbers. So there is life even down here, in the deepest part of the ocean.

like supporting the weight of a car on one fingernail! *Trieste* was designed to cope with this massive pressure. For years it was the only craft that could go so deep. But the small submersible on Guam has been built to do the same job. A U.S. Navy ship

Mission Debriefing

Diving to the midnight zone was exhausting work. It took a long time to get there, and you usually had to travel in a small, cramped craft. You may not have liked the feeling of being miles beneath the ocean surface. But the view out of the thick windows has always made the trip worthwhile.

On your journey you saw some amazing fish and other animals, including many that glow in the dark. You discovered how they find **prey** with their sharp senses and light tricks. And now you know how they use their big mouths and long teeth to catch prey.

In the North Atlantic Ocean you visited the giant wreck of the *Titanic,* lying deep in the midnight zone. You discovered how it sank in 1912, and what has happened to it during more than 90 years on the ocean floor.

In the **tropical** Pacific you investigated **seamounts,** and some of the life that lives near the ocean floor. And you took a trip to the deepest part of any ocean, anywhere on Earth. It has been an amazing journey.

Bioluminescent squid are just one kind of animal you saw in the ocean depths.

Glossary

absorb soak up

adaptation any special feature of a living thing that makes life easier or possible

antennae feelers that many animals use to sense movements in the air or water

bacteria very small living things that reproduce by splitting in two

basalt dark, heavy rock that forms most of the ocean floor

bioluminescence light produced by living things

bridge on a ship, the control center where the captain usually works

camouflage color or shape that makes an animal look like its surroundings

chart map of the seafloor and coast

colony group of living things that live together

compressed squashed

corals small, sea anemone-like animals

current flow of ocean water

debris wreckage and broken remains

equator imaginary line around the center of Earth, halfway between the North and South Poles

extinct no longer existing (little things), or no longer active (volcanoes)

freezing point temperature at which a liquid freezes into a solid

glaciers huge sheets of ice found in mountain valleys or very cold regions

hadal zone deepest zone of the ocean, only found in ocean trenches

luminous able to glow in the dark

lure bait that can be used again and again

microscope device for looking at things that are too small to see with the naked eye

mucus sticky fluid produced by animals

mutualism relationship between different species from which each organism benefits

nerves electrical network that carries signals between an animal's brain, senses, and other parts

organisms living things. All plants, algae, and animals are organisms.

organs parts of living things with special jobs to do. The heart and lungs are organs.

oxygen gas that all living things need to turn food into energy

photophores light-producing parts many deep-sea animals

plankton community of organisms that drifts in the ocean, mainly near the surface

predators animals that hunt, kill, and eat other animals

pressure squeezing force produced by a heavy weight

prey animals that are killed and eaten by other animals

ROV Remotely Operated Vehicle. It is a small underwater craft that is steered by someone sitting in another craft.

rusticles icicle-like growths made of rust and tiny living things. They form on iron in the deep ocean.

seamounts volcanoes that have erupted from the ocean floor, but have not grown tall enough to reach the surface

sonar device that locates solid objects by detecting reflected sound signals

sphere round ball shape

submersible small submarine designed for short trips. Some can dive to great depths.

tentacles long, flexible, sensitive "arms" used by squid to catch prey

thermocline boundary between two layers of water that have different temperatures

thermometer instrument that measures temperature

tropical of the tropics

tropics hot parts of Earth on either side of the equator

water pressure force of water pressing down on something

Books and Websites

Books

Marx, Christy. *Life in the Ocean Depths.*
New York: Rosen, 2003.

Pfeffer, Wendy. *Deep Oceans.* Tarrytown,
New York: Benchmark Books, 2002.

White, Katherine, and Earle, Sylvia.
Deep Sea Explorer and Ocean Activist.
New York: Powerkids Press, 2003.

Websites

www.bbc.co.uk/nature/blueplanet
The website of the BBC series about ocean
life, with extra information and games.

oceanexplorer.noaa.gov
The website of the U.S. National Oceanic
and Atmospheric Administration, about
the technology of ocean exploration
and ocean wildlife.

www.seasky.org/sea.html
A website packed with information
about the ocean.

www.titanic-online.com
An excellent website about the famous
wreck, with details of the ship, the sinking,
and expeditions to the ocean floor.

Index